# The Holy Face of Jesus Medal

William J. Timmerman, PhD

# The Holy Face of Jesus Medal

2019

Pen Shop Publishing

San Antonio, Texas

William J. Timmerman, PhD

# Table of Contents

# The Holy Face of Jesus Medal

# Introduction

"Lord, this is the people that longs to see your face"-
Psalm 24:6

The "Holy Face of Jesus" is a devotional centerpiece
that continues to grow in popularity among Christians.
When I first learned about it, I was led to a whole new
view of God's divine providence. What better way to
help us confront temptation to sin by having the face of
Jesus front and center and close to our heart. Let us
begin by looking at the earliest devotion to the "Holy
Face of Jesus."

The face of Jesus is the face of God as the second
person of the Trinity. There are no popular images of
the face of God the Father or the Holy Spirit that serve
as a center of devotion. Two separate images have
become the most popular and honored holy faces of
Jesus among Christians.

The Holy Face of Jesus

The Veil of Veronica is the oldest image that today continues to draw a very strong following. Tradition has it that when Jesus was forced to carry the cross on the way to his crucifixion, a woman in the crowd named Veronica rushed out and wiped the face of Jesus with a cloth of some type. It likely happened one of the times when Jesus had fallen to the ground from the weight of the cross. She used the cloth to wipe away the blood, sweat, dirt, spit and tears. The cloth miraculously was left with an image of his anguished face imprinted on it. The incident does not appear in the Bible but comes from a long-held tradition. The event is memorialized as the Sixth Station on the Way of the Cross.

The devotion to Veil of Veronica as the Holy Face of Jesus originated in 1844. Sister Marie of St. Peter, a French nun, reported a vision in which Jesus said to her, "Those who will contemplate the wounds on My Face here on earth, shall contemplate it radiant in heaven." She had more visions in which Jesus and Mary urged her to spread the devotion to the Holy Face of Jesus in reparation for the many insults Jesus suffered during his Passion.

Another French nun, the highly revered Saint Therese of Lisieux, also known as the "Little Flower", strengthened the call for devotion to the Holy Face of Jesus imprinted in the Veil of Veronica. She made up her own little prayer card with a small image of Jesus' face on it. She would later write her "Canticle to the Holy Face" that ended with "My love discovers the charms of Your Face adorned with tears. I smile through my own tears when I contemplate Your sorrows."

Later on, she composed the Holy Face prayer for sinners: "Eternal Father, since Thou hast given me for my inheritance the adorable Face of Thy Divine Son, I offer that face to Thee and I beg Thee, in exchange for this coin of infinite value, to forget the ingratitude of souls dedicated to Thee and to pardon all poor sinners."

More recently, devotion has developed in response to a second image of a "Holy Face of Jesus." The image is from the Shroud of Turin. The Veil of Veronica happened when Jesus was alive; the second Holy Face image comes from the burial cloth after his death called the Shroud. Both images are believed to have resulted from miraculous events. The Shroud of Turin image is due to a mysterious process that science still cannot fully explain. One reason is that the clearly visible image of the Holy Face of Jesus mysteriously appears on the photographic negative while the actual image on the cloth as seen with the naked eye is very faint and hard to make out. Somehow, some way the photographic negative is the much clearer image of the holy face.

Devotion to the Holy Face of Jesus whether it is depicted on the Veil of Veronica or the face on the Shroud of Turin shows the physical signs of the suffering he offered up for humanity and sadly the lack of consolation and thanksgiving for what he did for us. It is the same message that every apparition of the Virgin Mary gives to us whether at Fatima or Akita. That is, pray for the conversion of sinners and for God's protection from all the evil doings in the world resulting in wars, attacks on the Church, abortion, selective genocide and many other horrors and most of all, for the reparation for all the many offenses against God.

In 1936, Sister Maria Pierina De Micheli, an Italian nun, reported a vision in which Jesus told her: "I will that My Face, which reflects the intimate pains of My Spirit, the suffering and the love of My Heart, be more honored. He who meditates upon Me, consoles Me." Later she was instructed to have a medal made with the Holy Face of Jesus. On one side the medal bears a replica of the Holy Face image from the Shroud of Turin and an inscription based on Psalm 66:2: "Illumina, Domine, vultum tuum super nos", i.e. "May, O Lord, the light of Thy countenance shine upon us". On the other side of the medal, there is an image of a radiant Sacred Host, the monogram of the Holy Name ("IHS"), and the inscription "Mane nobiscum, Domine" i.e., "Stay with us, O Lord."

In another vision Jesus told her: "Every time my Face is contemplated, I will pour out my love into the heart of those persons, and by means of my Holy Face the salvation of many souls will be obtained."

From the stories of how the devotion to the holy face of Jesus came into being it is clear that both Jesus and the Virgin Mary asked for its creation.

# My Fascination with the Face of Jesus

I was graced with the opportunity to create A Quiet Place in Bryan, Ohio. It presented over two-hundred images of Jesus in paintings, plaques, statues and crosses in an art gallery setting to be used for prayer groups, religious program presentations and Christian counseling at no cost to the community.

It came into being as a result of two separate experiences. As the leader of a RCIA (Rite of Christian Initiation of Adults) program for local Catholic parishes, one of the topics I always reserved for myself was a presentation on the images of Jesus. In the beginning, I would layout a collection of holy cards of Jesus and ask the participants to select their top three favorites. Then they were asked to tell why they selected the ones they liked the most.

When A Quiet Place was created the little holy cards were replaced by big pictures and paintings of Jesus. And just like in the RCIA presentation, people who visited A Quiet Place were asked to pick out the images that spoke to them the most. I had my favorite. It was the Shroud of Turin. In fact, it had such a powerful impact on me I paid many dollars to have actual full-length replicas of both the positive and negative images of the Holy Shroud at A Quiet Place. The positive image was laminated so visitors could come up and touch the blood stains or some other aspect on the image and surrounded on the wall with plush velvet draping all along the edges of a 14 foot by 4-foot rectangular frame. Moreover, it was flanked by two seven-foot-tall back-lighted negatives of the Shroud (frontal and dorsal images).

I was fully up to date on the most recent scientific research findings which served me well during the question and answer sessions following the formal presentation. When the word got out, churches asked if youth groups could come to see the Shroud presentation. That was fine. There was no charge. With time, seven to eight adult prayer groups met regularly at A Quiet Place.

Whenever I had free time between my appointments for Christian counseling sessions at A Quiet Place, I would relax in front of the Shroud. Often, I meditated on that phrase in the Apostles' Creed "(He)…suffered under Pontius Pilate, was crucified, died and was buried." The Shroud made that phrase so powerfully alive for me knowing all that Jesus suffered for me and all of us. And, as someone told Angela, my good friend in Italy, "Contrition means standing in front of the cross (in this case the Shroud) and saying admittedly, 'And this is how I treated you!'"

The first time I saw the actual Shroud of Turin was in 1978. I immediately knew in my heart it was the actual burial cloth of Jesus Christ. As soon as I returned home, I developed a four-projector slide show that I presented many times in Northwest Ohio and one time in Italy. As I write this, there is a small picture of the face of Jesus from the Shroud on my desk. It is called a 3D holographic picture that when you turn it slightly from side to side the face changes from a death mask to a fully alive face. The picture serves as a constant reminder of the price He paid and the special place He has in my life and for my family.

# The Shroud of Turin

When Pope John Paul II visited the Turin Cathedral in 1998, he said: "The Shroud is an image of God's love as well as of human sin" and "it is an icon of the suffering of the innocent in every age."

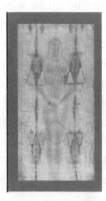

I first heard about the Shroud at a party when a person I never met before happened to mention it to me. He steered me to an article in the Toledo Blade Sunday magazine insert. It described the Shroud and noted that it would be on exhibit in Turin, Italy the next year in 1978.

At the same time there was an Italian exchange student named Angela who was in a small prayer group at our church we became friends with. When it was time for her to return to Italy, she said something like "come and see me sometime". Little did I know at the moment that everything eventually would come together in short order with God's help so we could travel to Italy on vacation and see the Shroud of Turin.

I'll never forget my first glimpse of the Shroud as I entered out of the bright sunlight into the dimly lit Cathedral of John the Baptist in Turin, Italy. A religious service was going on. The music was quietly reverent and somber like background music in a mortuary. I immediately sensed that I was in the presence of something very holy and emotionally moving. As I sat off to the side toward the back of the church, I could not take my eyes off of the center of attraction in a far off back-lighted case and began saying to myself how thankful I was to be in the presence of the shroud of Jesus. I had absolutely no doubt what I was seeing had not only actually been touched by Jesus but had wrapped his dead body.

Suddenly I felt someone in back of me moving my wheelchair and turned to see it was an usher. I already was quite satisfied with my view of the Shroud but now he was moving me closer to the image. He placed me in the line that would take me within just twelve feet of the Holy Shroud. I sat mesmerized with eyes fixed on the beautiful image of his body while saying out loud, "Thank you, Lord" over and over again while tears cascaded down my face. When it was time for the line to move, I craned my neck to look over my left shoulder as long as I could knowing without any question that Jesus had left the one and only photograph of him as he lay in a death position.

Twenty years later I saw the Shroud of Turin again. I would see it the third time in 2000.

During the return visit to Italy in 1998 my friend Angela arranged for me to visit a little museum near the Shroud Exposition to meet with the director of the International Center of Sindonology in Turin, Italy. However, Dr. Bruno Barberis was unavailable while we were there. Angela managed to talk to his secretary for Dr. Barberis to call me at a designated time in the evening. That evening we had dinner in Florence in a lovely restaurant with a group of Angela's friends. They were a joyful, boisterous bunch, and everyone seemed to have a cell phone. At the scheduled time I borrowed one of their phones and went off to a fairly quiet corner in the restaurant.

I soon found out from Dr. Barberis he was a professor of rational mathematics, an expert in statistics and probability. He seemed insulted when I asked his view on the authenticity of the Shroud. He was quick to remind me that he was a scientist. He said he had computer generated the probability of the Shroud being someone other than Jesus.

He broke down the chances using some of the specific aspects of the Shroud as they related to the passion, crucifixion, and burial. The probabilities were based on excavation of crucifixion victims, and Jewish customs and practices at that time. For example, the probability of the wound in the side found on the Shroud was calculated as a one-in-ten chance. This is because the typical Roman death blow to a crucifixion victim was to

13

break their legs to hasten asphyxiation. Wounds in the head from a cap of thorns was estimated at 1-in-5000. How many crucifixion victims would have had crowns placed on their heads? According to Dr. Barberis, when seven aspects of the Shroud are combined, the probability of the man of the Shroud being someone other than Jesus Christ was estimated at: one in 200 billion!

I did not need Dr. Barberis to tell me who the man of the Shroud is. I already knew.

# The Power of the Visual

*A picture is worth a thousand words*

Research indicates that visual cues are much better in getting our attention, enhancing memory retrieval and increasing retention compared to verbal information. Indeed, a picture is worth a thousand words. In today's digital age we are bombarded every day with visual imagery more so than ever before.

"Visuals are processed 60,000 times faster than text"- Baris Gencel

With the expansion of secularism an increasing number of people are distancing themselves from religion which closes the gap between the natural world and the spiritual realm. Religious imagery is fading from public consciousness. This is unfortunate because the only real truths rely on supernatural content. Religious images facilitate the relationship with the transcendent and provide mutual interactions between human beings and the divine. A votive image of Jesus like the "Holy Face of Jesus" merges the material reality of the image and the reality of his presence in our lives.

When I was a little boy, I would visit from time-to-time Grandma and Grandpa Timmerman's house in Newport, Kentucky. I still can see in my mind the many religious pictures and statues all around their small house. As a little kid having Jesus and saints look at me created in me a more reverent, mannerly, and calming effect unlike when I visited Grandma and Grandpa Frick's house. There I would run around and "get into everything." I will never forget I stole two little magnetic toy dogs that I kept despite feeling guilty about it. I would never have stolen anything from the Timmerman's. My point is that the religious images in the house in Newport had a definite effect on my behavior. It was like being in a church.

That experience as a little boy has helped convince me of the potential power religious visual images can have on you and me. It is wonderful some people have developed special prayers and devotional practices to carry out in honor of Jesus' face. What I have discovered is that an image of Jesus can instantly get my attention and remind me of his actual presence in my life.

Recently when going down a highway, I saw this big semi-truck go by with a gigantic picture on the side of the truck advertising delectable Hostess Cupcakes covered with delicious chocolate icing and the creamy white stuff in the middle. I immediately thought of how long it had been since I had one to enjoy. Then, I thought why don't we buy them anymore? I need to remind myself the next time I go shopping to get them, but so far it hasn't happened.

When is the last time you have seen a rainbow? What associations did you immediately think of? Maybe it's the pot of gold and the little lepercon it leads to or "whenever the rainbow appears in the clouds, I will see it and remember the everlasting covenant between God and all living creatures of every kind on the earth" (Genesis 9:16). Notice how fast we can connect a rainbow to either a religious or non-religious theme.

I ran across a blog attached to a "holy face of Jesus" devotional website. It read "Print the little icon of the Holy Face and put it everywhere-so it's the first thing you see in the morning and the last thing at night. And over the sink, by the computer, on the dashboard, by the inside of the front door." That got me thinking. Why not strategically locate it in the place where the occasion of sin tempts me the most? It's hard to give into sin when Jesus is looking you in the face.

For example, place his image right next to the computer or as the wallpaper on your computer. Or, maybe have it on the mouse pad. Why? To counteract the temptation to search for pornography or wasting too much idle time looking at ads instead of accomplishing something worthwhile.

If you have a habit of gossiping put an image of Jesus as the opening screen on your cell phone. Here are more:

- If it is a problem with road rage, spewing angry curse words at other drivers or cell phone usage while driving which is against the law, have the face of Jesus as first screen on the cell phone or put an image on the dashboard or on a steering wheel knob.

17

- If alcohol problems, put a picture of Jesus on top of the liquor cabinet or a magnet on the refrigerator.

- I have a picture of Jesus Divine Mercy that is the first image I see when I open my billfold instead of my ID. Why? To help me curb my spending. The credit card by the way is harder to get to.

You have the idea now and can decide how the image of Jesus can help you to resist the type of temptation that bothers you the most. If not sure of yours, go down a list of the seven capital sins or the Ten Commandments while you examine your conscience. You and me, like everybody else, has at least one brand of sin that needs confrontation and control.

The earlier blog presented a great practice. Put a picture of Jesus just inside the front door. That way we can be sure to say "Good morning, Jesus" or later on, when we go out to face the "world, the flesh and the Devil" as a reminder of the need for his protection. And, we cannot forget to say "Good night" to him before going to bed.

Recently I forgot the practice of saying an evening prayer before bed that includes a brief review of the day and my good and my not so good behavior. I now have a picture of the face of the Shroud right next to my computer that I shut down before going to bed. I'll see if that helps. Another way is to have an image of Jesus on the nightstand next to the bed.

You may want to have your favorite image of the Virgin Mary or a favorite saint in a place that is easy to see. That is fine idea too. But the emphasis in this book is on the "face of Jesus".

If God is for us, who can be against us? It is easy to see how an image of Jesus can remind us that he is with us and who is against us- the evil creature called the Devil.

I know how it affects me whenever I gaze at the picture of Jesus on my desk. I cannot understand how a person can look at a picture of the Holy Face and at the same time give into temptation. Even if the temptation to sin is extremely strong one glance at the face of Jesus should counter the sinful thoughts for most people. The face of Jesus says to me when I look at it, "It is either me or the Devil, the choice is up to you."

# The Power of the Holy Face of Jesus Medal

Devotions to the Holy Face were approved by Pope Leo XIII in 1895 and Pope Pius XII in 1958.

I wear the little medal of Jesus' face on the Shroud around my neck. I have been doing this for many years now. I believe the image of Jesus helps protect me from evil wherever I am. For me, it is a very good thing to do.

I pray that the power of the Holy Face of Jesus leads to more and more devotees. I'm afraid too many people do not understand its powerful impact on helping them refrain from giving into the temptation to sin.

Almost every learned prayer is aimed at protecting us from sinning. The Lord's Prayer ends with "lead us not into temptation but deliver us from evil. Amen." The Hail Mary Prayer ends "pray for us sinners now and at the end of our lives. Amen." The Prayer to Michael the Archangel includes "Defend us in battle. Be our safeguard against the wickedness and snares of the Devil." These prayers are said with our lips or in our head. The great benefit of having a Holy Face of Jesus medal in view or resting over your heart is it enlivens your prayer to include your physical senses of sight and touch. It is one thing to talk to God, it is even better to "see" God and to "feel" God by means of the holy face medal.

We are all addicts in the real sense of the word. We can become addicted to any of the seven deadly sins. The first addictions we tend to think about are alcohol abuse, unfettered gambling, illicit drug addiction or addiction to pornography. Some people are addicted to gossiping, hoarding or lying and cheating. We are all sinners and have our own Achilles' heel of vulnerability to certain sins. Psalm 51:11-14 speaks to my sinfulness: "Dear Lord",

Turn away your face from my sins;
    blot out all my iniquities.
A clean heart create for me, God;
    renew within me a steadfast spirit.
Do not drive me from before your face,
    nor take from me your holy spirit.
Restore to me the gladness of your salvation;
    uphold me with a willing spirit.

You and I can be continually reminded of God's constant presence in our lives by an image of the Holy Face of Jesus medal.

I hope and pray that everybody who reads this will have or obtain and keep a holy face of Jesus medal very close to them. Maybe it will be on a chain around one's neck like mine, on a bracelet around their wrist or at least on a key chain to protect them against all evil.

And for you dear reader, I pray,

*May "The LORD make His face shine on you and be gracious to you; (may) the LORD turn His face toward you and give you peace." Numbers 6:25-16*

Please visit the appendix for a sample of prayers you might care to use. If you want a free medal and prayer cards, visit my Ebay site titled *saintpedro*. Look for the heading for the ad, "Shroud of Turin Medal & 2 Prayer Cards". Use "contact seller" and give me your name and address. No charge for shipping.

Thank you and may God bless you abundantly.

# More Jesus Medals

# Bibliography

Blessed Maria Pierina de Miceli, The Holy Face com.

Badde, Paul. The Face of God. Ignatius Press, San Francisco, 2006.

Blessed Maria Pierina de Miceli, The Holy Face com.

Buechner, Frederick. The Faces of Jesus-A Life Story, Paraclete Press, Brewster, Massachusetts, 2006.

Malacaria, Davide. Mother Pierina and the Face of Jesus, 30 Days in the Church and the World, issue no. 01/02 – 2011.

Rigamonti, Sister Maria Ildefonsa. The Story of Sister Maria Pierina de Michaeli, HFA.

The Holy Shroud and Four Visions, TAN Books and Publishers, Rockford, Illinois, 1974.

"The Life of Leon Papin-Dupont," (ed. Edwin H. Thompson), Library of Religious Biography, Volume VIII, Chapter 1, Burns and Oates, 1882.

The New American Bible, Revised Edition (NABRE). World Bible Publishing, March 9, 2011.

Timmerman, William. The Holy Face of Jesus Medal, Kindle, 2019.

Wuenschel, E.A. Self-Portrait of Christ: The Holy
Shroud of Turin, Holy Shroud Guild: Esopus NY,
Third printing, 1961.

# Prayers

### Prayer to Saint Michael the Archangel

"Saint Michael, the Archangel, defend us in battle;

be our protection against the wickedness and snares of the devil.

May God rebuke him, we humbly pray, and do thou, O prince of the heavenly host,

by the power of God, thrust into Hell, Satan and all the other evil spirits,

who prowl throughout the world, seeking the ruin of souls. Amen."

### Prayer of Saint Alphonsus Liquori

"My most beloved Jesus, Thy face was beautiful before, but in this journey it as lost all its beauty, and wounds and blood have disfigured it. Alas! My soul also once was beautiful, when it received Thy grace in Baptism, but I have disfigured it since by my sins. Thou alone, my Redeemer, canst restore it to its former beauty. Do this by Thy Passion, O Jesus."

### The Golden Arrow Prayer

May the most holy, most sacred, most adorable, most incomprehensible and ineffable Name of God be forever praised, blessed, loved, adored, and glorified in heaven, on earth and in hell, by all the creatures of God, and by the Sacred Heart of Our Lord Jesus Christ in the Most Holy Sacrament of the Altar. Amen.

### Prayer of Pope Pius IX

O Jesus! Cast upon us a look of mercy; turn Thy Face towards each of us as Thou didst to Veronica; not that we may see it with our bodily eyes, for this we do not deserve, but turn it towards our hearts, so that, remembering Thee, we may ever draw from this fountain of strength the vigor necessary to sustain the combats of life. Amen. Mary, Our Mother, and Saint Joseph, pray for us.

### Special Prayer

Most Holy Face of Jesus, we are truly sorry that we have hurt Thee so much by constantly doing what is wrong; and for all the good works we have failed to do. Immaculate Heart of Mary; Saint Joseph, intercede for us, help us to console the Most Holy Face of Jesus. Pray that we may share in the tremendous love Thou hast for one another and for the most Holy and Blessed Trinity. Amen.

### Prayer of Blessed Maria-Pierina

O Blessed Face of my kind Savior, by the tender love and piercing sorrow of Our Lady as she beheld you in your cruel Passion, grant us to share in this intense sorrow and love so as to fulfill the holy will of God to the utmost of our ability. Amen.

# Other Books by William Timmerman on Amazon

Our Mother Mary's Warnings at Civitavecchia, Akita, Garabandal and Fatima

Our Lady of Civitavecchia

Is God Using UFOs?

Your Guardian Angel: Things You Maybe Didn't Know

Where the Hell Did "Hell" Go?

The Scary Warning from Garabandal

The Spiritual Power of Acronyms Workbook

Spiritual Microchips: How to Access Yours

In 2034 Anti-Christianity Triumphs in America

Am I Crazy or Just Senile?

Who Is "Angel Phanuel"?

America Doesn't Love Children

Can the Devil Read Our Minds?

Offering It Up for Souls and the World

Suffering and Spirituality: My Story

My Funny Toilet Tales

Adjustment to Work: Using A Questionnaire for
Interview Purposes

Bless Me and Break All Curses on Me

Understanding Work Adjustment

Needs and Empowerment

Mania, Meniah and Me

God's Gift of Hands

The Gifts of Children: How They Touch Our
Hearts and Souls

God's Gift of Our Marvelous Hands

America's Children in the 21st Century-A Call to
Action

The Journey in Becoming a Lowly Person

Uh, Uh, Satan! You Had Me for a While but No
More

Made in United States
Troutdale, OR
12/20/2023

16295455R00033